COLOR BETWEEN THE VINES

A Vine-inspired coloring book

"Look at all those chickens!" (@lookatallthosechickens)

"This kid's definitely on crack right now..." (Nate Moszyk)

DAMN DANIEL

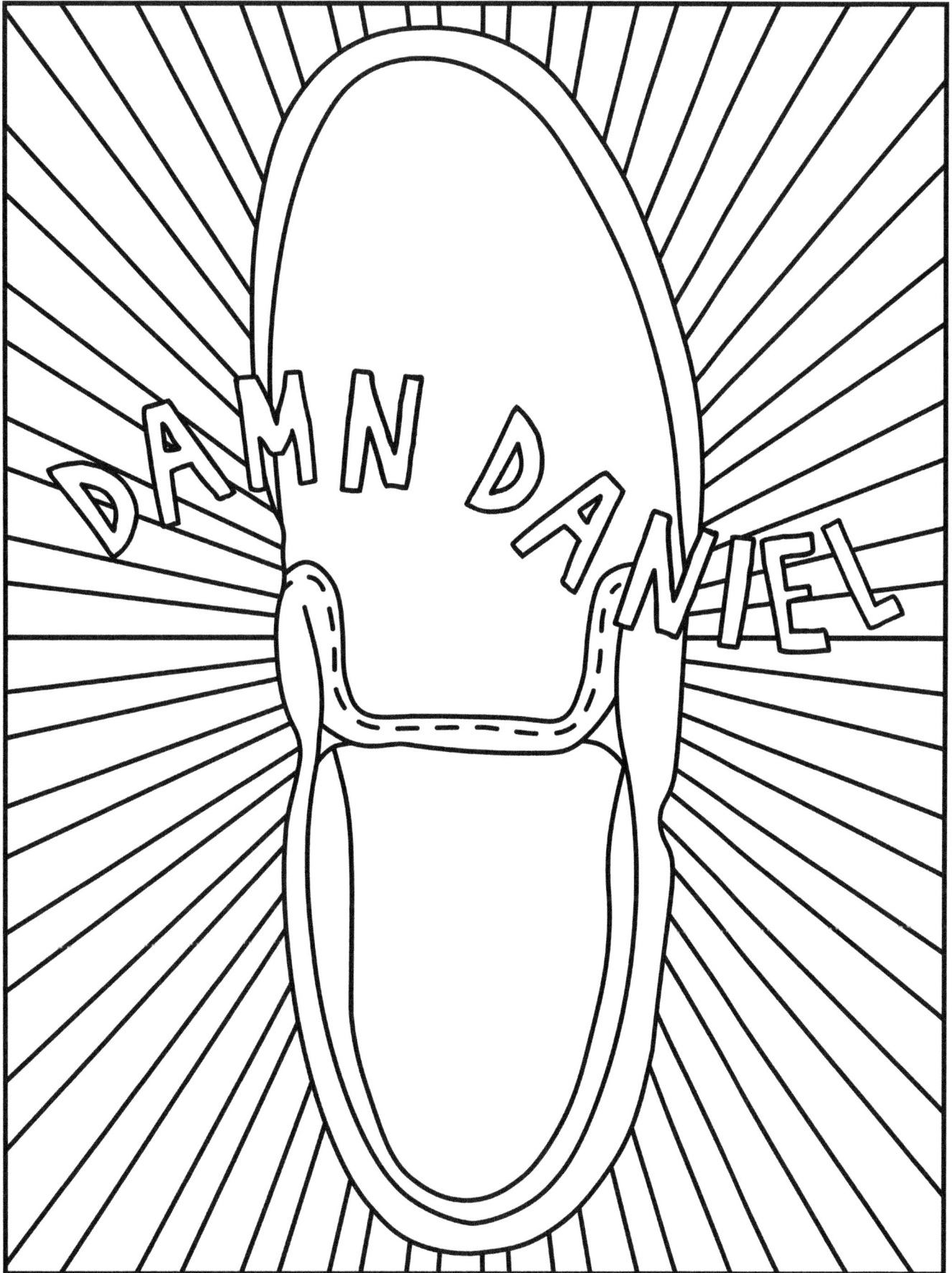

"Back at it again with the white vans!" (Josh Holz)

The worst Jamaican accent. Ever.

"Hi, welcome to Chili's." (Adam Perkins)

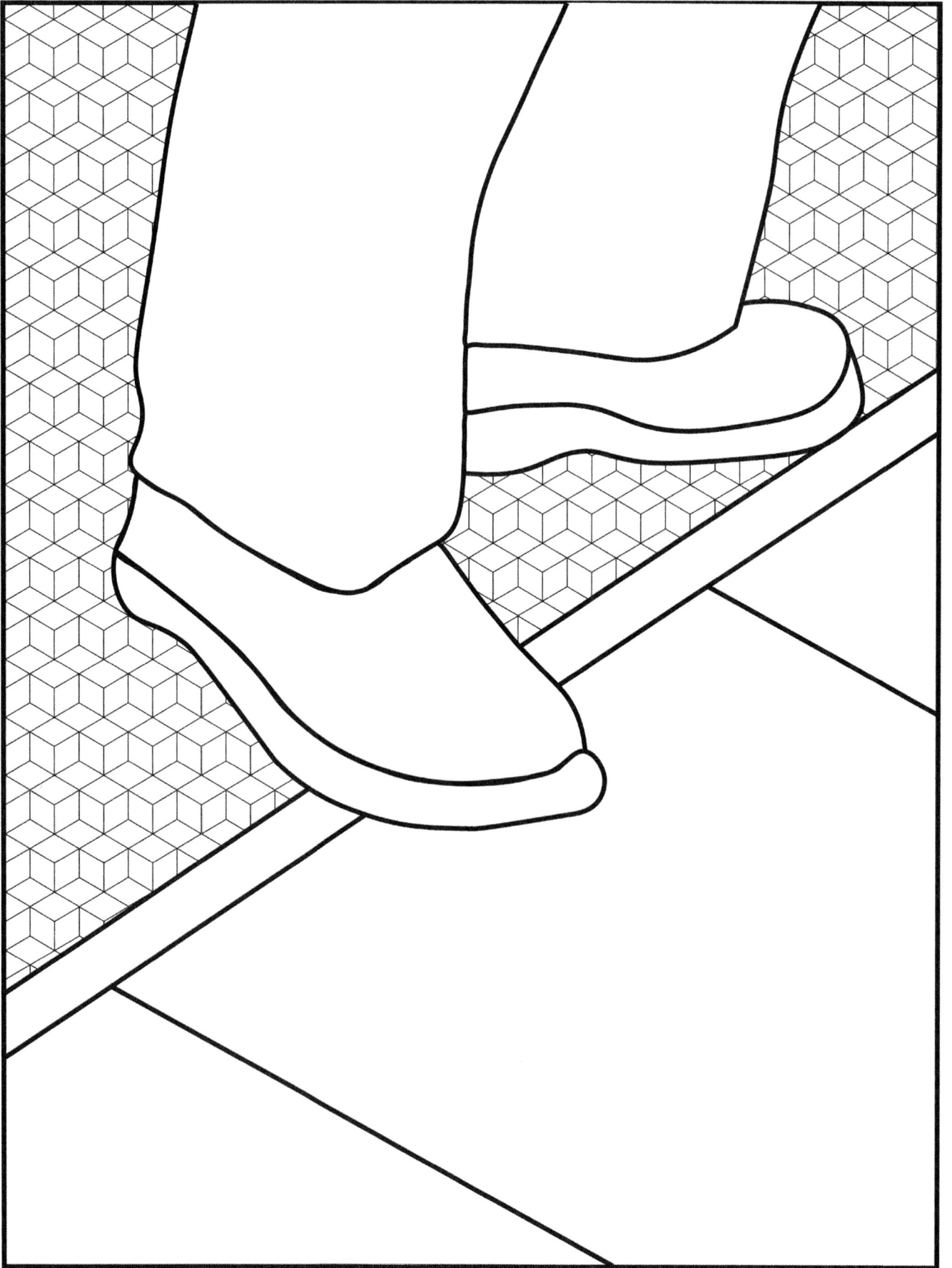

"WHAT ARE THOSE!!!" (A-RODney King)

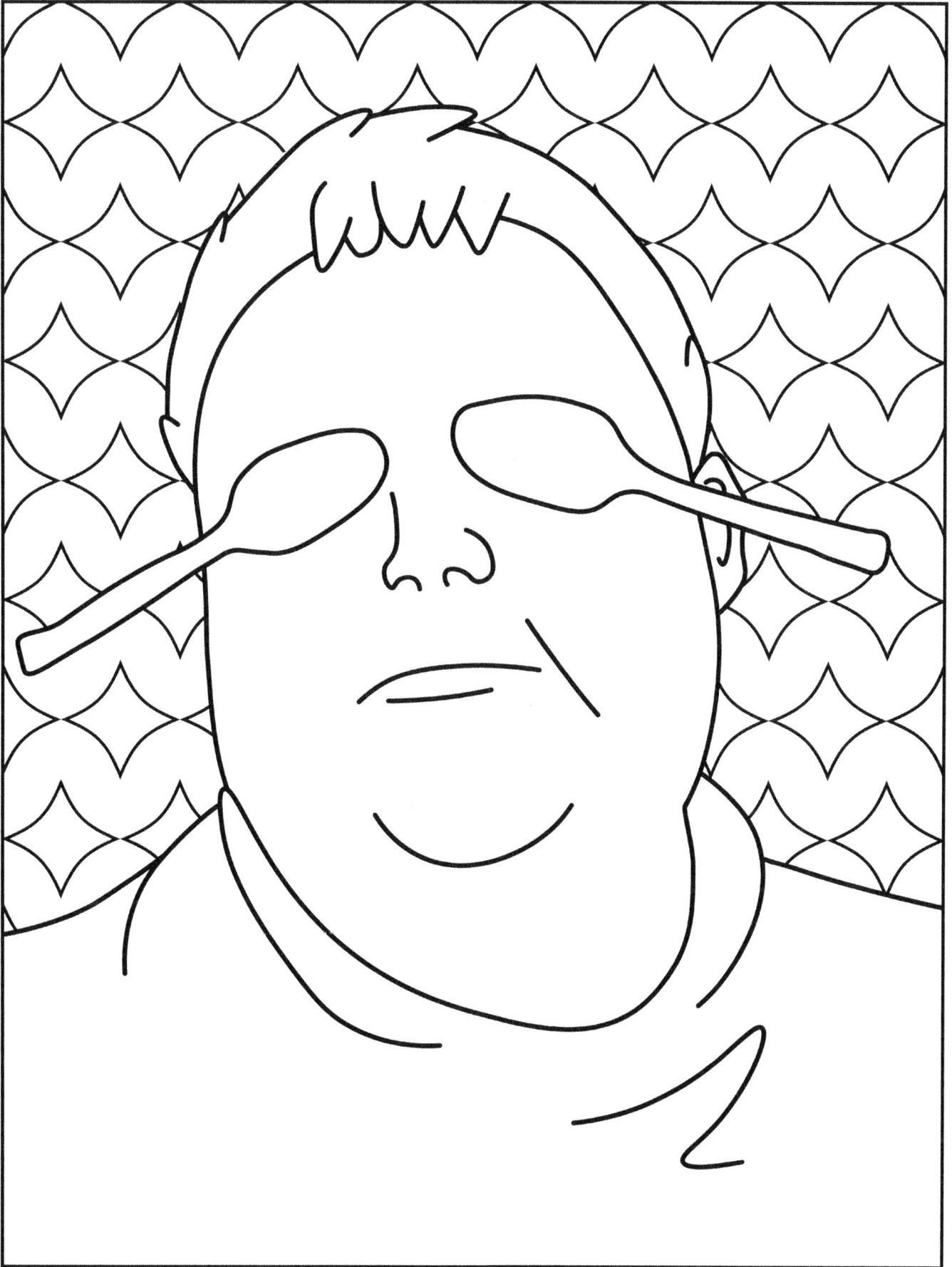

"Hi I'm sorry I didn't see you there, I was too busy blockin' out the haters." (Brandon Bowen)

"YAAAAS!" (Blake Welch)

"My snickers my snickers?" (Curtis Lepore & Christian Delgrosso)

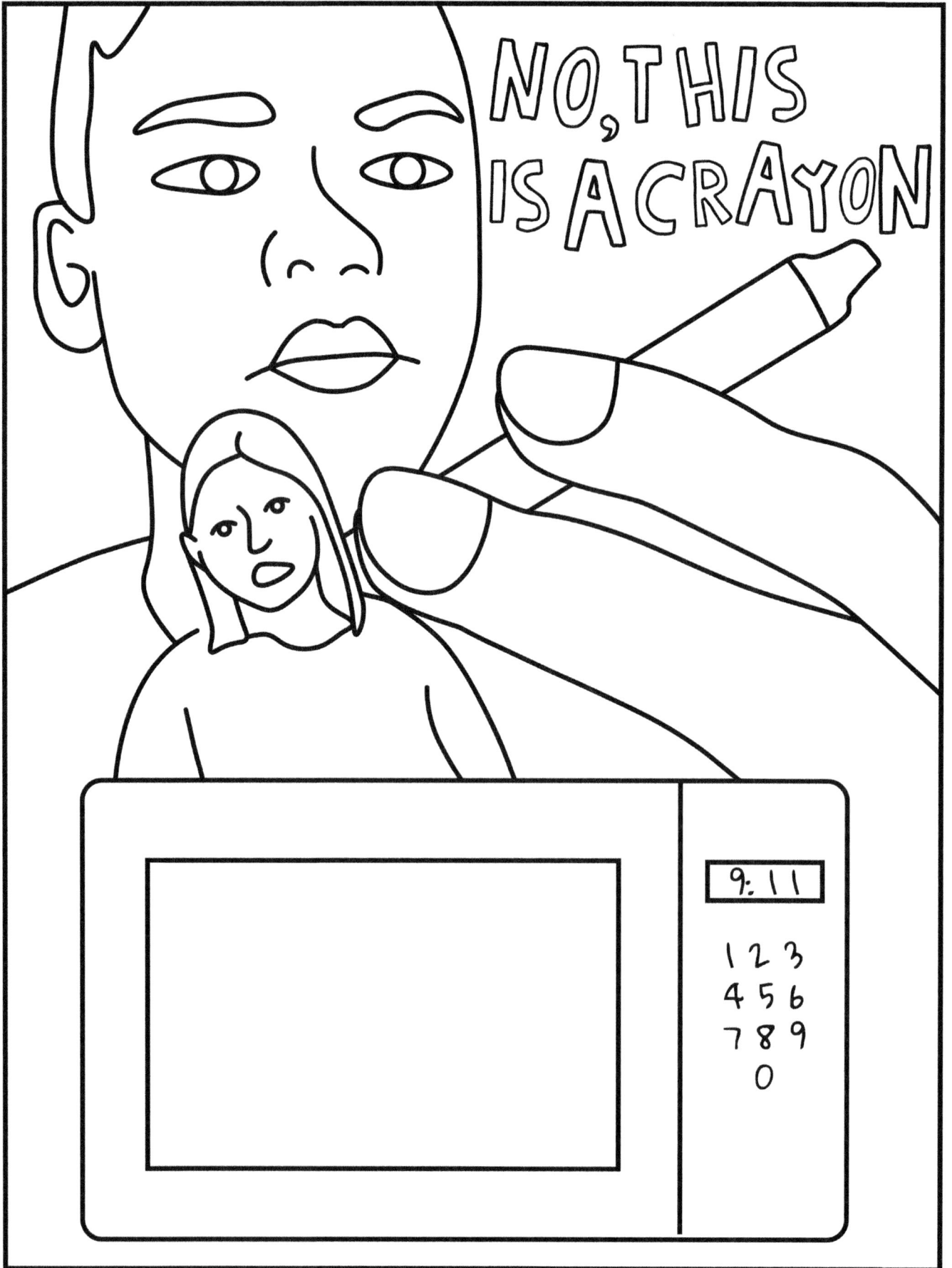

"Is that a weed?!" (Chris & Red Robyn)

"It's an avocado..." (Jeffery Walter)

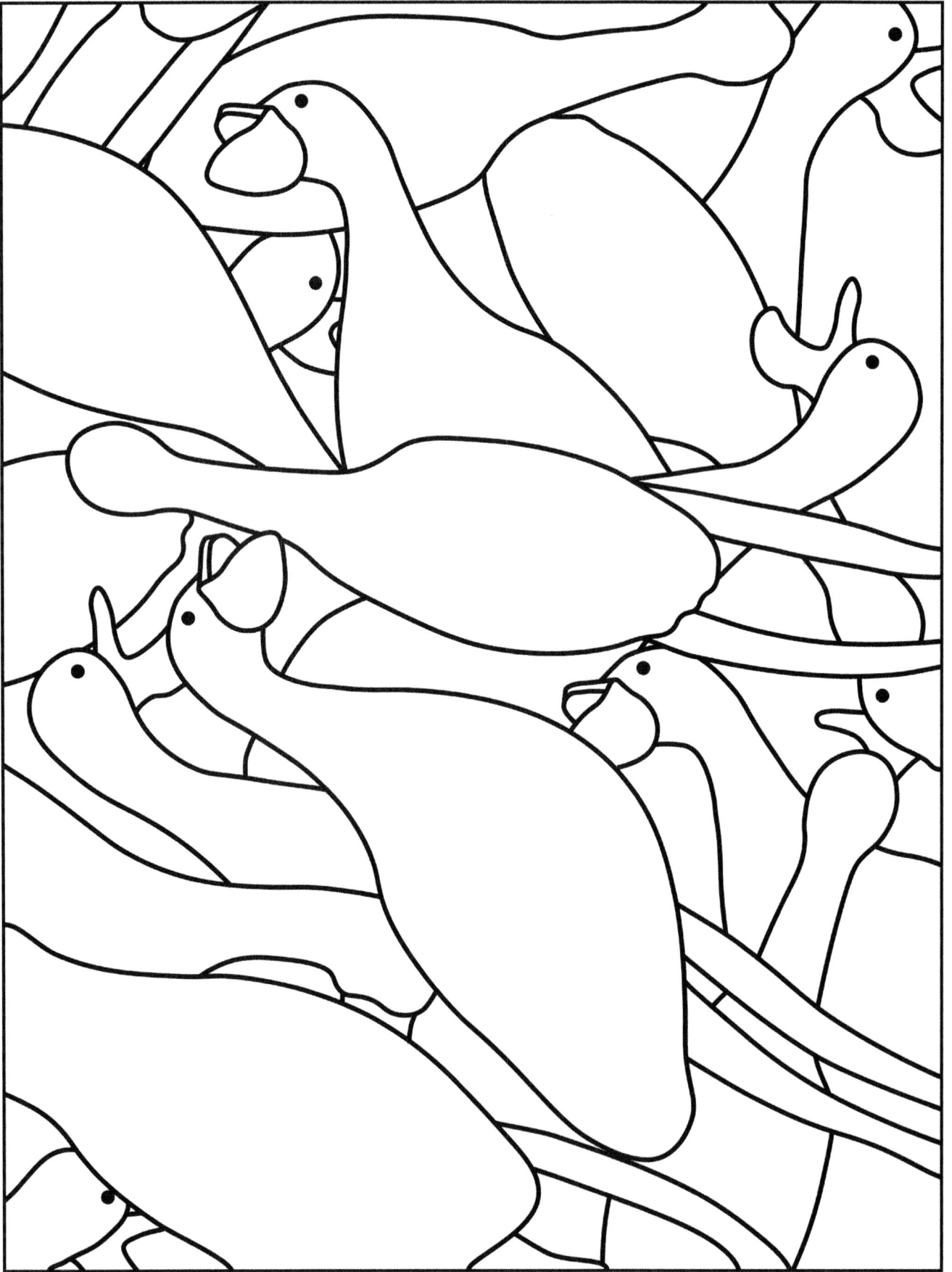

Loud plastic duck squeaking (Kevin Synnes)

"The gallon joust!" (@snowboardjacket)

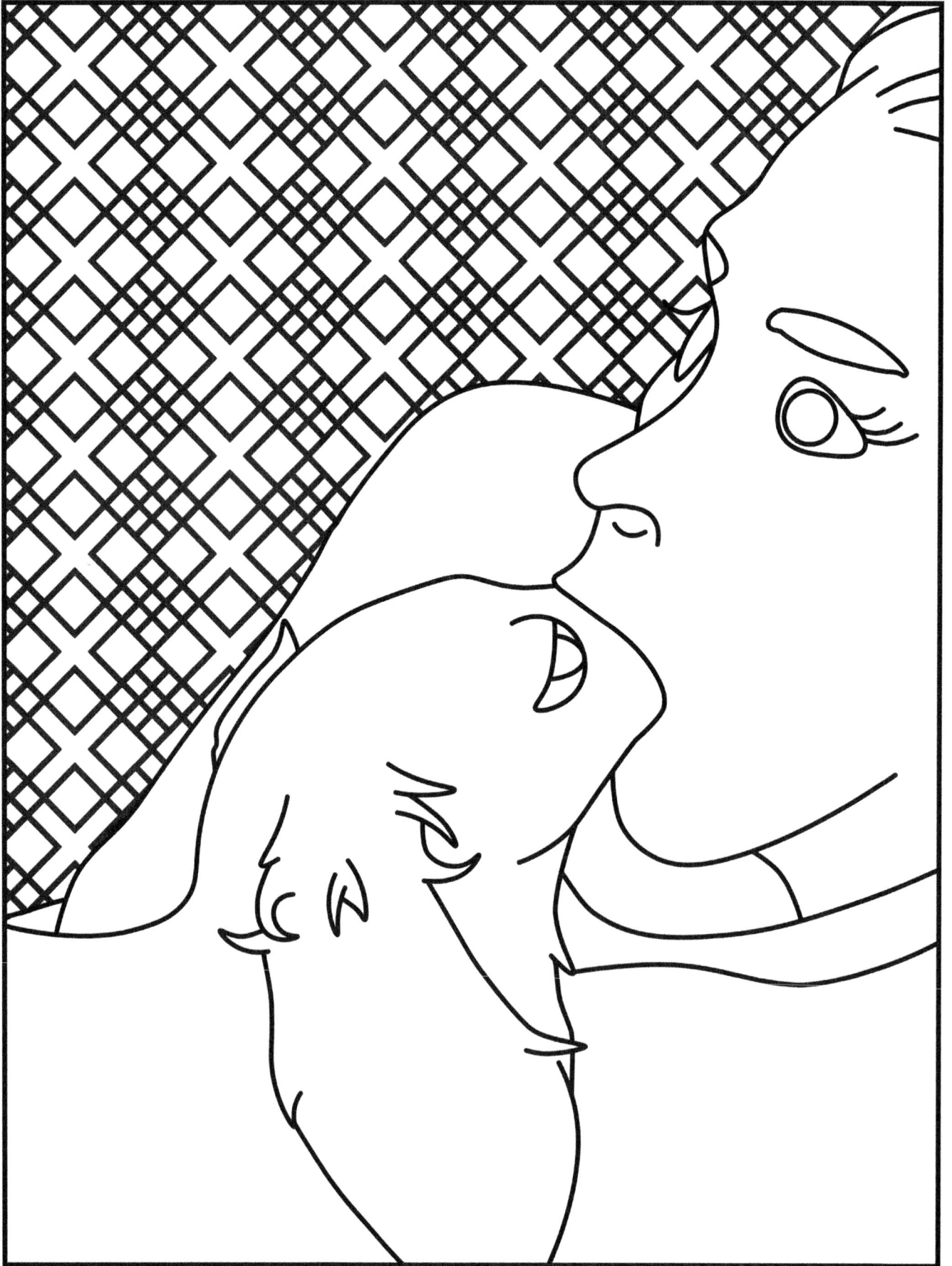

"Baaaaaa!" *shushed* (Brittany Furlan)

"Do it for the vine!" (Diamonique Shuler)

Who is she? (Chloe Woodard)

"THAT I COULD WALK INTO THE STORE AND GET THE PART!" (Porscha Coleman)

"Why you always lyin'?" (@downgoes.fraser)

"I tapped the breaks…" (Lauren Lavoie)

"A potato flew around my room." (PG Bree)

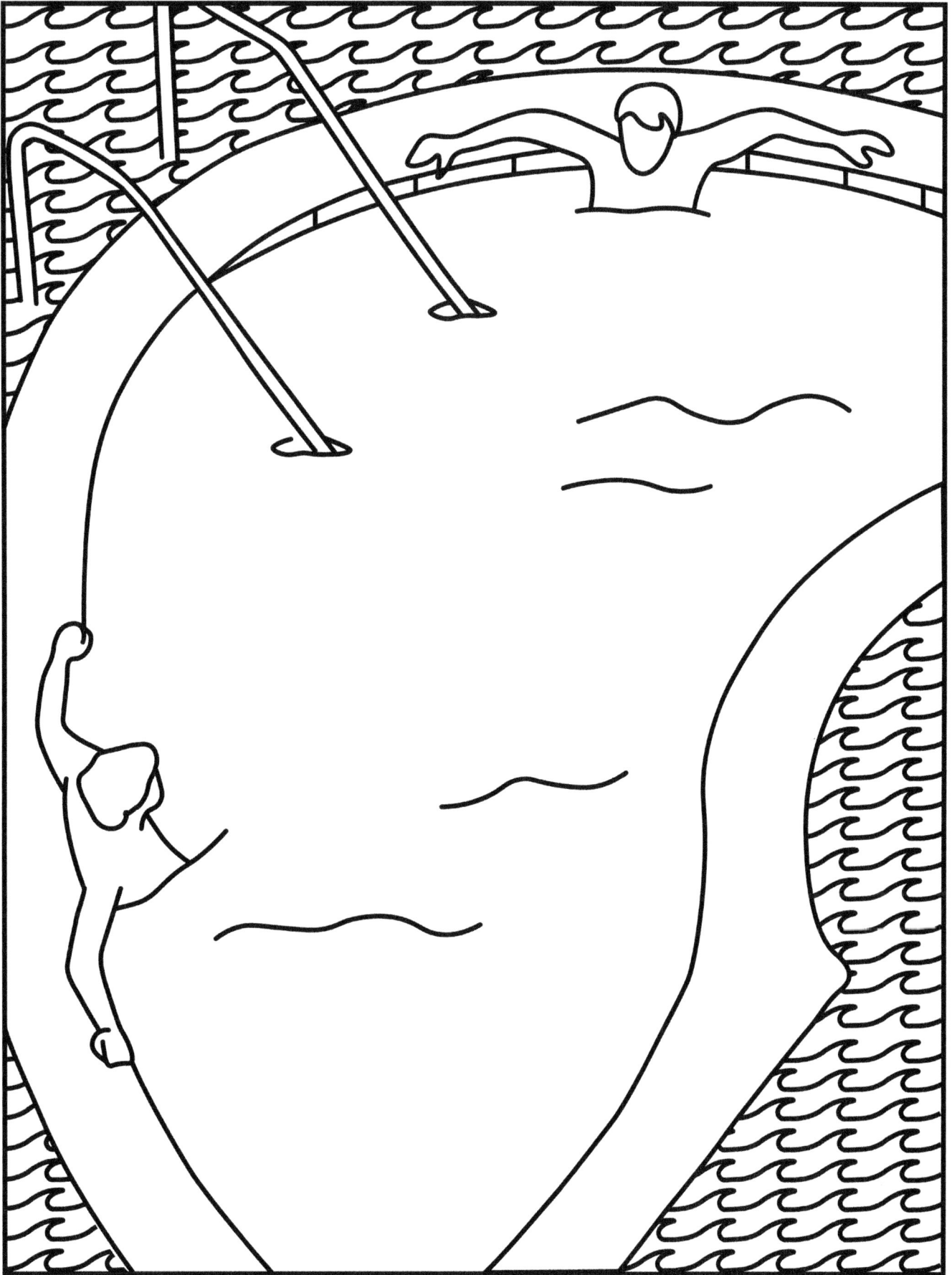

"Two bros chillin' in a hot tub five feet apart 'cause they're not gay." (Anthony Padilla)

"Hey. I want to be famous." (Rachel Olson)

Printed in Great Britain
by Amazon

35965532R00020